Horses of the Air

Written by Sheila Kelly Welch

CelebrationPress

An Imprint of ScottForesman
A Division of HarperCollinsPublishers

Flying Horses!

Can horses fly? Don't answer
that question too quickly!
You might have seen pictures
of horses with wings.
Sometimes on a starry night
you can see a flying horse.
His name is *Pegasus*. You
have to look very hard
in the night sky and use
your imagination.

Of course, Pegasus is not a real horse. You cannot ride a horse made of stars. You cannot *gallop* through the clouds on a horse that is just in your imagination.

But there are real horses who seem to fly. They leap high into the air. These horses are called *Lipizzans*, and their history is very interesting.

The history of the Lipizzans began more than four hundred years ago in Austria. At that time, people used horses during battles. They needed horses that were strong and fast.

The Austrian archduke Karl decided to start a farm in a village called Lipizza to raise warhorses and carriage horses for his stables. He brought horses from Spain to help start a new type of horse, or breed. They called the horses Lipizzans.

Although they came from several breeds, all Lipizzans are related to one of the first six Lipizzan *stallions*. Even now, every *colt*'s name is created using one of the names from the first six horses.

Conversanc

Favory	Siglavy	Maestoso	Neapolitano	Pluto

**Pluto III
Amerita**

Wars often put the Lipizzan horses in danger. Sometimes they had to be moved from place to place to protect them from harm. People in Austria call these horses their "national treasures."

Today, Lipizzans live and perform all over the world.

General George Patton

Lipizzan foals are dark when they are born. Most of them turn white as they get older.

Lipizzan *foals* spend their time running and playing, eating and sleeping. At first, they stay close to their mothers for milk and safety. But soon, the foals make friends with all the others. Just like all horses and children, a Lipizzan foal enjoys lots of company.

Lipizzans start school when they are four years old. At first, they must learn very simple things, such as how to walk slowly with a trainer and to stop and stand still.

Some of the *fillies* are trained to pull carriages. Many of them will become mothers and have foals of their own.

When the colts are big and strong enough, they are ready to begin to learn the movements that make the Lipizzans famous.

A trainer works slowly and gently with the stallions. He starts each horse on a long rope called a *longe line*. He uses this to teach the horse to listen and follow commands.

Young stallions go to school for a whole year before they perform in front of people. Their training continues for many years. Each horse is different and can do some things better than others. Only a few are able to perform the most amazing movements, called the *"Airs Above the Ground."*

Lipizzans are gentle and are very good students.

Lipizzans have been performing all over the world for hundreds of years. They have been in circuses, horse shows, and the Olympic Games. Each summer, the horses at Tempel Farms near Chicago perform for hundreds of people. The performances are much like those seen in Austria.

Getting the Lipizzans ready for a performance is a lot of work. They must be washed, brushed, and dressed up. The horses appear to dance when they enter the ring. They move together, doing the same high steps that Lipizzans did long ago. All their movements are full of power and beauty.

If you look up into the deep, dark night sky, you might find Pegasus among the stars. But here on earth, you can meet horses that jump so high that they seem to fly.

That is why the Lipizzans can be called "Horses of the Air."

Glossary

"Airs Above the Ground": unusually high leaps performed by the Lipizzans

colts: young male horses

fillies: young female horses

foals: all young horses, both male and female

gallop: a fast, natural three-point gait (movement) of a horse

Lipizzans (also called Lipizzaners): a breed of horse from Austria that is noted for its beauty and ability to do many special movements

longe line: a long, flexible line that is used for exercising and training horses before they are ridden

Pegasus: a winged horse from a Greek myth and a constellation of the same name

stallions: male horses that are able to sire (father) foals